ROSEN ✔ *Verified*

U.S. GOVERNMENT

SEPARATION OF POWERS

Daniel R. Faust

ROSEN
PUBLISHING

New York

Published in 2021 by The Rosen Publishing Group, Inc.
29 East 21st Street, New York, NY 10010

First Edition

Editor: Siyavush Saidian
Book Design: Reann Nye

Photo Credits: Cover (Supreme Court Building, White House) Orhan Cam/Shutterstock.com; cover (Capitol Building) Orhan Cam /Shutterstock.com; Series Art PinkPueblo/Shutterstock.com; p. 5 WINDN/ASSOCIATED PRESS; p. 7 serato/Shutterstock.com; p. 8 DEA PICTURE LIBRARY/ De Agostini/Getty Images; p. 11 National Galleries of Scotland/ Hulton Fine Art Collection/Getty Images; p. 12 https://commons.wikimedia.org/wiki/File:Scene_at_the_Signing_of_the_Constitution_of_the_United_States.jpg; p. 13 Jack R Perry Photography/Shutterstokc.com; p. 14 Daniel Lange/Shutterstock.com; p. 16 mark reinstein/Shutterstock.com; p. 19 Evan El-Amin/Shutterstock.com; p. 20 Patsy Lynch/MediaPunch/IPx/AP Images; p. 21 Fine Art/ Corbis Historical/Getty Images; pp. 22–23 Travel Stock/Shutterstock.com; p. 24 https://commons.wikimedia.org/wiki/File:John_Marshall_by_Henry_Inman,_1832.jpg; p. 25 Drew Angerer/Getty Images News/Getty Images; p. 27 Library of Congress/Hulton Archive/Getty Images; p. 28 Alex Edelman/Getty Images News/Getty Images; p. 30 mark reinstein/Shutterstock.com; p. 31 Chris Maddaloni/ CQ-Roll Call, Inc./Getty Images; p. 33 Three Lions/ Hulton Archive/Getty Images; p. 35 Historical/Corbis Historical/Getty Images; p. 37 Rob Crandall/Shutterstock.com; p. 39 Orhan Cam/Shutterstock.com; p. 41 WPA Pool/ Getty Images Entertainment/Getty Images; p. 43 Hector Vivas/ Getty Images News/Getty Images; p. 45 Rischgitz/ Hulton Archive/Gety Images.

Library of Congress Cataloging-in-Publication Data

Names: Faust, Daniel R., author.
Title: Separation of powers / Daniel R. Faust.
Description: New York : Rosen Publishing, [2021] | Series: Rosen verified:
    U. S. government | Includes index.
Identifiers: LCCN 2020006040 | ISBN 9781499468670 (library binding) | ISBN
    9781499468663 (paperback)
Subjects: LCSH: Separation of powers–United States–Juvenile literature. |
    United States–Politics and government–Juvenile literature.
Classification: LCC JK305 .F38 2021 | DDC 320.473/04–dc23
LC record available at https://lccn.loc.gov/2020006040

Manufactured in the United States of America

Some of the images in this book illustrate individuals who are models. The depictions do not imply actual situations or events.

CPSIA Compliance Information: Batch #BSR20. For Further Information contact Rosen Publishing, New York, New York at 1-800-237-9932.

Find us on

CONTENTS

The History of Separation 4

From Ancient Greece to the Enlightenment 6

Branches of Government 8

Checks and Balances 10

The U.S. Constitution 12

The Legislative Branch 14

The Powers of the Legislative Branch 16

The Executive Branch 18

The Powers of the Executive Branch 20

The Judicial Branch 22

The Powers of the Judicial Branch 24

Legislative Checks and Balances 26

Executive Checks and Balances 28

Judicial Checks and Balances 30

Necessary and Proper 32

Executive Orders 34

More Checks and Balances 36

Separation of Powers Around the World 38

The British System 40

The Mexican System 42

Truly Balanced? 44

Glossary 46

Index 48

THE HISTORY OF SEPARATION

Imagine living during the European Middle Ages. You wouldn't have had any control over the laws you had to follow. The people who made and **enforced** the laws wouldn't care if you thought they were unfair. The governments of the Middle Ages were autocratic. This means that power was held by a single person or group.

Today, we know that this is unfair. Many of the world's governments today are republics. In a republic, the people elect **representatives**. These representatives make the laws and run the government. The leaders in a republic can be unfair too, however. How do you make sure that one part of the government doesn't get too powerful? One way is to separate power between different branches, or parts.

Hundreds of years ago, nobles and monarchs wrote the law. The average person had very little say in how the government was run.

FROM ANCIENT GREECE TO THE ENLIGHTENMENT

The idea of separating parts of a government has been around for a long time. The Greek **philosopher** Aristotle described the idea of a "mixed government" in the fourth century BC. Aristotle wrote about a government that contained three parts. The first part was the monarch, or the king. The second part was the aristocracy, or the wealthy class. The third part was the democracy, or the people.

FRIENDS! ROMANS!

The Roman Republic was governed by three branches.

- **The Senate:** These seats were inherited by the wealthy.

- **The Assembly:** These members were elected by the people.

- **The Consuls:** These leaders were elected to limited terms by the Senate.

Our idea of democracy is based on the political system of the ancient Greek city-state Athens. In ancient Athens, laws were created by the Assembly. All free landowning males were allowed to speak and vote in the Assembly.

ENLIGHTENED GOVERNMENT

During the Age of Enlightenment (1685–1815), Aristotle's "mixed government" idea was updated. John Locke believed a fair government would be made up of a lawmaking branch and a head of state. In 1748, French philosopher Montesquieu added the idea of a court system. This is the three-branch system the United States uses today.

BRANCHES OF GOVERNMENT

Enlightenment-era philosophers influenced the U.S. Founding Fathers. When they created a new government for the United States of America, they made sure no single group would have too much power. They created a government with multiple branches. Each branch was given **specific** powers. The U.S. government has three branches. These are the legislative branch, the executive branch, and the judicial branch.

Before writing the U.S. Constitution, the Founding Fathers wrote the Articles of Confederation. The federal government created by the Articles of Confederation was too weak. The country needed a better option.

THREE BRANCHES OF GOVERNMENT

LEGISLATIVE BRANCH

The U.S. Congress; includes the Senate and the House of Representatives

POWERS:
Makes laws

EXECUTIVE BRANCH

The head of state; includes the president, vice president, and most federal agencies

POWERS:
Enforces laws

JUDICIAL BRANCH

The Supreme Court and other federal courts

POWERS:
Decides trials that involve federal laws; decides if laws violate the Constitution

 **VERIFIED**
You can read more about the powers and duties of the U.S. government's three branches here:
https://www.usa.gov/branches-of-government

CHECKS AND BALANCES

American colonists believed the British monarchy was too powerful. That's what started the American Revolution. The Founding Fathers didn't want that to happen to their government. They came up with a way to distribute power between three branches. Each branch has powers that the others don't. This is called a system of checks and balances. It means no single branch should be more powerful than the others.

England's King George III was considered an unfair ruler. The Founding Fathers wanted to make a new government that would be more fair to Americans.

THE U.S. CONSTITUTION

The U.S. Constitution was signed on September 17, 1787. It created the federal government still in power today. The Constitution has seven articles, or sections. The first three articles created the three branches of the federal government. The Constitution also includes the Bill of Rights. The Bill of Rights are the first 10 **amendments** made to the Constitution. The Bill of Rights gives rights and freedoms to everyone in the United States.

Several of the Founding Fathers refused to sign the Constitution unless it included the Bill of Rights.

THE SEVEN ARTICLES OF THE U.S. CONSTITUTION

Article I: Created the U.S. Congress.

Article II: Created the office of the president.

Article III: Created the Supreme Court of the United States.

Article IV: Defined the relationship between the federal government and the state governments.

Article V: Gave Congress the ability to amend the Constitution.

Article VI: Stated that the U.S. Constitution is "the law of the land."

Article VII: Listed all of the people who signed the U.S. Constitution.

 **VERIFIED**

You can read the entire Constitution on the National Archives website:
https://www.archives.gov/founding-docs/constitution-transcript

THE LEGISLATIVE BRANCH

Article I of the U.S. Constitution created the legislative branch. The legislative branch is also called the U.S. Congress. Congress is responsible for making our country's laws. Congress has two chambers, or houses. One house is called the Senate. The other is called the House of Representatives. Both houses work together to create and pass laws. Senators and representatives are elected directly by the American people.

The U.S. Capitol has been home to the U.S. Congress since 1800. Known for its famous dome, the Capitol contains both chambers of Congress, as well as offices and meeting rooms.

ONE CONGRESS, TWO HOUSES

THE SENATE

100 members

Each state elects two senators.

Elected for a term of six years.

Must be at least 30 years old.

Must have been a U.S. citizen for at least nine years.

Led by the president pro tempore of the Senate.

THE HOUSE OF REPRESENTATIVES

435 members

The number of representatives for each state is based on the population.

Elected for a term of two years.

Must be at least 25 years old.

Must have been a U.S. citizen for at least seven years.

Led by the Speaker of the House.

THE POWERS OF THE LEGISLATIVE BRANCH

The main job of Congress is making the country's laws. A bill can be **proposed** by either house. When both houses agree on the bill, it's sent to the president. The president can either sign or **veto** the bill. If a bill is signed by the president, it becomes law. The Constitution gives Congress many other powers. The Senate and the House of Representatives share many of these powers. Other powers are given to one house but not the other.

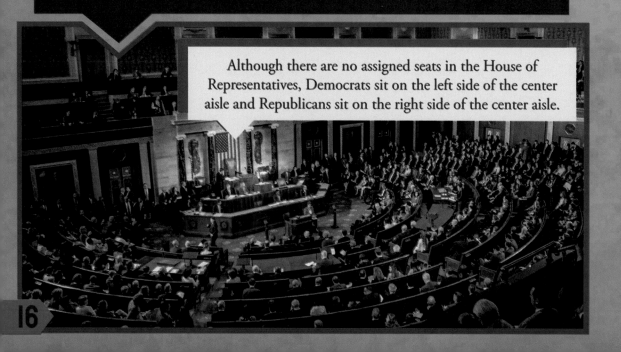

Although there are no assigned seats in the House of Representatives, Democrats sit on the left side of the center aisle and Republicans sit on the right side of the center aisle.

THE POWERS OF THE U.S. CONGRESS

POWER	THE SENATE	THE HOUSE OF REPRESENTATIVES
Pass laws	X	X
Amend the Constitution	X	X
Raise taxes		X
Confirm presidential appointments	X	
Ratify treaties	X	
Declare war	X	X
Elect the president in case of a tie		X
Elect the vice president in case of a tie	X	
Impeach a federal officer		X
Hold trials for impeached officials	X	

✔ VERIFIED

You can learn more about Congress at the official website:
https://www.congress.gov/

THE EXECUTIVE BRANCH

The executive branch was created in Article II of the Constitution. The main job of the executive branch is to enforce laws passed by Congress. The head of the executive branch is the president. The president is also the head of state and the leader of the federal government. The executive branch also includes the vice president, the president's cabinet, 15 executive departments, and other government agencies.

THE CABINET

The cabinet gives the president advice on important issues. Members of the cabinet include the vice president, the heads of the 15 executive departments, and heads of other important federal agencies.

The Seal of the President of the United States is the official symbol of the presidency. The stripes on the shield represent the 13 original states and the ring of 50 stars represents the current 50 states. The olive branch and the arrows stand for peace and war respectively.

THE 15 EXECUTIVE DEPARTMENTS

- Department of Agriculture
- Department of Commerce
- Department of Defense
- Department of Education
- Department of Energy
- Department of Health and Human Services
- Department of Homeland Security
- Department of Housing and Urban Development
- Department of Justice
- Department of Labor
- Department of State
- Department of the Interior
- Department of the Treasury
- Department of Transportation
- Department of Veterans Affairs

THE POWERS OF THE EXECUTIVE BRANCH

As the head of the federal government, the president has a lot of responsibilities. The Constitution gives the president the powers they need to do their job. The president is the commander-in-chief of the military. The president **conducts** relations with foreign countries. That includes making treaties. When there's a position available in the federal government, the president decides the person they want to fill that position. This power is used to appoint heads of government agencies, **ambassadors**, and federal judges.

The Constitution says that the president must give a speech to both houses of Congress once every year. This is called the State of the Union address. The speech typically includes a report on the economy and what the president wants to accomplish in the coming year.

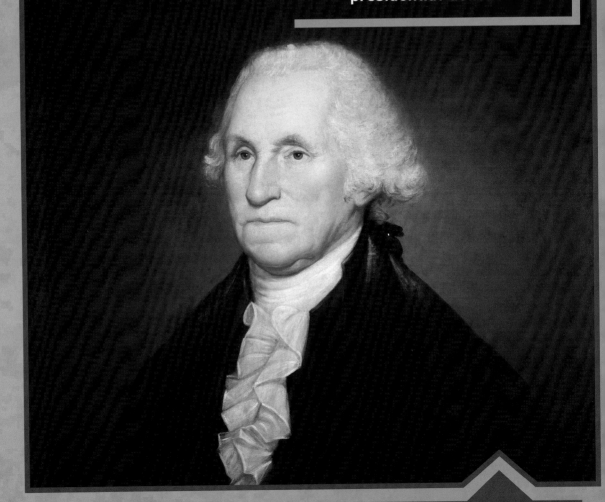

THE FIRST PRESIDENT

When the U.S. Constitution was written, most countries were ruled by kings or emperors. The idea of a president was new. Many presidential traditions began with the first president, George Washington. Washington didn't want the presidency to be like the monarchies of Europe. To avoid this, Washington asked to be addressed as "Mr. President," instead of "Your Excellency" or "Your Highness."

THE JUDICIAL BRANCH

The judicial branch was created by Article III of the Constitution. This branch includes the Supreme Court and other federal courts. The Supreme Court is at the top of the judicial branch. It's also the highest court in the country. There are nine judges on the Supreme Court. They're called justices. The leader of the Supreme Court is called the chief justice. A Supreme Court justice is chosen by the president. They serve until they die, **retire**, or resign.

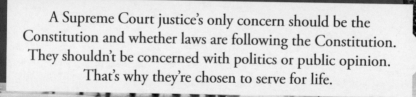

A Supreme Court justice's only concern should be the Constitution and whether laws are following the Constitution. They shouldn't be concerned with politics or public opinion. That's why they're chosen to serve for life.

THE POWERS OF THE JUDICIAL BRANCH

The Constitution gives the judicial branch a lot of power. Courts have the **authority** to decide cases that affect federal law. They also look at disagreements between states. Federal courts rule on cases between people who live in different states. Most cases are handled by the federal courts. If one side is unhappy with a **verdict**, they can challenge it. This is called an appeal. Most Supreme Court cases are appeals from lower courts. The Supreme Court mainly hears cases that involve important legal principles.

John Marshall

John Marshall was the fourth chief justice of the U.S. Supreme Court. He was appointed in 1801 and served until 1835. Chief Justice Marshall is largely responsible for the role the Supreme Court has in today's federal government. His decisions increased the power of the judicial branch, making it the equal of the other two branches.

The Constitution states that the chief justice must preside over any presidential impeachment trials. In January 2020, Chief Justice John Roberts presided over the impeachment trial of President Donald Trump.

LEGISLATIVE CHECKS AND BALANCES

The Constitution gives Congress many powers. It has many ways to balance the other two branches. Congress has the authority to confirm, or agree to, presidential appointments. The president has the power to create treaties with other countries. However, these treaties must be ratified, or approved, by the Senate. Congress also decides how much money to give the federal government each year.

OTHER CHECKS AND BALANCES

The Constitution also gives Congress these powers to check the other branches:

• Create amendments to the Constitution

• Increase or decrease the number of justices on the Supreme Court

• Create federal courts

Andrew Johnson was the first of three presidents to be impeached by the House of Representatives. In March 1868, the House charged him with "high crimes and misdemeanors." The Senate didn't convict him.

EXECUTIVE CHECKS AND BALANCES

The Constitution lets the executive branch appoint judges. They work in federal courts or the Supreme Court. This allows the president to fill the judicial branch with people who agree with them. The executive branch balances the legislative branch with veto power. If the president doesn't like a bill, they can veto it. A vetoed bill goes back to Congress. It's either rewritten or it fails.

Congress has the power to override, or ignore, a presidential veto. If two-thirds of the members of both houses vote to ignore the veto, the bill becomes a law without the president's signature.

THE MOST PRESIDENTIAL VETOES

(1789–2008)
Some presidents have vetoed hundreds of bills.
Some barely vetoed any.

FRANKLIN D. ROOSEVELT — 635 vetoes
GROVER CLEVELAND — 584 vetoes
HARRY S. TRUMAN — 250 vetoes
DWIGHT D. EISENHOWER — 181 vetoes
ULYSSES S. GRANT — 93 vetoes
THEODORE ROOSEVELT — 82 vetoes

POCKET VETO

The president has 10 days to sign or veto a bill. If the president does nothing in that time, the bill is automatically rejected. This is called a pocket veto.

JUDICIAL CHECKS AND BALANCES

The judicial branch has the power of judicial review. Judicial review means federal courts can say a law is unconstitutional. That means that it **contradicts** the Constitution. This also applies to policies and other actions. Part of judicial review requires that the courts study the Constitution. They have to interpret what the Founding Fathers meant. The judicial branch uses judicial review to interpret laws written by Congress. Judicial review can also be used to declare an action taken by the executive branch unconstitutional.

The 1954 ruling in the case of *Brown v. Board of Education of Topeka* illustrates that the Constitution is a living document. It was designed to change and grow over time, just like society changes and grows.

IMPORTANT SUPREME COURT CASES

- **Marbury v. Madison (1803):** Determined that the Supreme Court had the power to declare a federal law or action unconstitutional.

- **McCulloch v. Maryland (1819):** Ruled that Congress had implied powers not originally stated in the Constitution.

- **Plessy v. Ferguson (1896):** Ruled that racial segregation was legal as long as it was "separate but equal."

- **Brown v. Board of Education of Topeka (1954):** Reversed the ruling of *Plessy v. Ferguson* and declared segregation illegal.

- **Miranda v. Arizona (1966):** Ruled that the police must inform suspects of their rights before questioning them.

NECESSARY AND PROPER

The U.S. Constitution gives Congress many powers. Some of its abilities are called expressed powers. These powers are specifically named in the Constitution. They include making laws, raising taxes, and declaring war. Congress also has implied powers. These aren't written in the Constitution. Implied powers are things Congress needs to do its job. Article I includes something called the necessary and proper clause. It's also called the elastic clause because it gives Congress **flexibility**. It also stretches Congress's power.

THE FIRST BANK

Congress created the Bank of the United States in 1791. Many people were against it, including Thomas Jefferson. Alexander Hamilton believed that Congress had the power to create a national bank. He claimed that because Congress had the power to raise taxes and borrow money, it also had the power to create a bank. Hamilton was using the necessary and proper clause to argue his point.

This drawing from around 1795 shows President Washington (right) speaking to two members of his cabinet: Thomas Jefferson (left) and Alexander Hamilton (center).

BASIC DISAGREEMENT

Thomas Jefferson and Alexander Hamilton disagreed on the nature of the federal government. Jefferson believed that the states should have more power than the federal government. Hamilton believed that a strong federal government would protect law and order.

EXECUTIVE ORDERS

The executive branch can't make laws. The president can propose laws. They can set a political **agenda**. The president can also decide to sign a bill or veto it. However, only Congress has the power to make new laws. A president can issue an executive order, though. Executive orders give instructions to the departments and agencies of the federal government. They can describe how to enforce laws and handle certain situations. Like laws, executive orders may be declared unconstitutional by the Supreme Court.

KEY EXECUTIVE ORDERS

- **Executive Order 6102 (1933):** President Roosevelt makes it illegal for private citizens to own gold coins or bars.

- **Executive Order 9066 (1942):** President Roosevelt orders the imprisonment of Japanese immigrants and Japanese American citizens during World War II.

- **Executive Order 9981 (1948):** President Truman ends racial segregation in the U.S. military.

- **Executive Order 10730 (1957):** President Eisenhower ends racial segregation of public schools.

Many people are afraid that executive orders can be abused. They believe that a president could use them to make laws. This would be a violation of the Constitution.

MORE CHECKS AND BALANCES

Checks and balances don't only exist between the branches of the government. The legislative branch can check and balance itself. Congress checks its own power by having two houses. Each house has different responsibilities and rights. Congress has other **internal** checks as well. One is that a bill passed in the House of Representatives must be the same as the one passed by the Senate. This keeps one house of Congress from adding something to a bill that's already been voted on by the other house.

THE 25TH AMENDMENT

The 25th Amendment provides an internal check on the powers of the executive branch. This amendment allows the vice president and the cabinet to vote on whether or not they believe the president is able to perform the needed duties. If they vote no, the vice president becomes the acting president.

Members of the House of Representatives are elected to directly represent specific areas of a state. Senators, however, represent their entire state.

SEPARATION OF POWERS AROUND THE WORLD

The United States isn't the only country that has different branches of government. The constitutions of many countries create governments with two or more branches. A system of government with three branches is most common. France, India, and Italy all use three branches of government. Some countries have governments with more than three branches. Some countries have as many as six divisions.

OTHER BRANCHES

Executive, legislative, and judicial are the most common types of branches of government found in other countries. In some countries, some powers held by one of these branches are given to a separate branch. Some of these other branches include:

- **Auditory:** A branch that makes sure the government is run efficiently and effectively.

- **Electoral:** A branch that is responsible for running a country's elections.

- **Prosecutory:** A branch that handles a country's law enforcement.

- **Civil service commission:** A branch that oversees civil servants and other nonelected government employees.

In the United States, federal law enforcement is handled by the Department of Justice. The Department of Justice is part of the executive branch. In some countries, law enforcement is handled by its own branch.

THE BRITISH SYSTEM

The British system of government has several different names. It's called the parliamentary or Westminster system. Like the U.S. system, the British government has a legislature made up of two houses. The House of Commons has members who are elected from 646 **districts**. The House of Lords is made up of members of the aristocracy. They commonly inherit their seats. The executive branch includes a prime minister and a cabinet. The prime minister is the head of the federal government. The judicial branch has no power to review laws.

In the United States, the president is both the leader of the federal government and the head of state. In the British system, the prime minister is the head of the federal government. The head of state is the monarch. As of January 2020, Great Britain's head of state is Queen Elizabeth II.

THE MEXICAN SYSTEM

Like the United States government, the Mexican government has three branches. The president of Mexico is the head of the executive branch. The judicial branch is divided into four separate parts. The Supreme Court of Justice is at the top. The legislative branch is called the General Congress. It has two houses: the Senate and the Chamber of Deputies. Each Mexican state has four seats in the Senate. Membership in the Chamber of Deputies is based on population.

Andrés Manuel López Obrador was elected president of Mexico in December 2018. In Mexico, the president can't be reelected. A president can serve for only one six-year term.

TRULY BALANCED?

The Founding Fathers had many goals when they wrote the Constitution. They did their best to make sure that no part of the government had too much power. They guessed that the legislative branch would be the most powerful. That's why there are many checks on the powers of Congress. Over time, the other branches became equally powerful. John Marshall's time as chief justice gave the judicial branch the power of judicial review.

Presidents like Franklin D. Roosevelt expanded the powers of the president. Are the three branches still balanced? Has one branch become more powerful than the others? These are questions politicians ask every day. In general, the separation of powers in the United States has been successful. Most people believe the three branches are fairly equal.

During the American Civil War, Abraham Lincoln
assumed more powers than any president before him.
He ignored Congress on many occasions.

GLOSSARY

agenda: A list of things to be considered or done.

ambassador: An official representative or messenger, especially to another country.

amendment: A change in the words or meaning of a law or document, such as a constitution.

assume: To take or have the ability to do something.

authority: The power to give orders or make decisions.

conduct: To plan or do something.

contradict: To deny or disagree with what someone or something is doing or saying.

district: An area established by the government for official government business.

enforce: To make sure that people do what is required by law.

flexibility: The ability to change or do different things.

internal: Existing or occurring within an organization.

philosopher: A person who studies philosophy, or the study of the basic ideas about knowledge, right and wrong, reasoning, and the value of things.

propose: To suggest to a person or group of people to consider something.

representative: A person chosen in an election to act or speak for the people who elected them.

retire: To stop a job or career after reaching a certain age.

specific: Clearly and exactly presented or stated.

verdict: The decision made by a jury or judge in a trial.

veto: To officially refuse to allow a bill to become a law.

INDEX

A
Aristotle, 6, 7

C
Chamber of Deputies, 42
Cleveland, Grover, 29
Congress, U.S., 9, 13, 14, 15, 16,
    17, 18, 20, 26, 28, 30, 31, 32,
    33, 34, 36, 40, 45

E
Eisenhower, Dwight D., 29, 34
Elizabeth II, Queen, 40
England, 10
executive order, 34, 35

F
France, 38

G
General Congress, 42
George III, King, 10
Grant, Ulysses, 29

H
Hamilton, Alexander, 32, 33
House of Commons, 40
House of Lords, 40
House of Representatives, 9, 14, 15,
    16, 27, 36, 37

I
India, 38
Italy, 38

J
Jefferson, Thomas, 32, 33
Johnson, Andrew, 27
judicial review, 30, 38, 44

L
Lincoln, Abraham, 45
Locke, John, 7

M
Marshall, John, 24, 44
Mexico, 42

O
Obrador, Andres Manuel Lopez, 42

R
Roberts, John, 2
Roosevelt, Franklin D., 29, 34, 44
Roosevelt, Theodore, 29

S
Senate, 6, 9, 14, 15, 16, 26, 27, 36,
    42
Supreme Court, 9, 13, 22, 23, 24,
    26, 28, 30, 34
Supreme Court of Justice (Mexico),
    42

T
Truman, Harry S., 29, 34
Trump, Donald, 25

W
Washington, George, 21, 33